A
SECOND
CHANCE
AT
Love

A SECOND CHANCE AT *Love*

MATTHIAS DEMO

authorHOUSE®

AuthorHouse™
1663 Liberty Drive
Bloomington, IN 47403
www.authorhouse.com
Phone: 1-800-839-8640

Published by AuthorHouse   06/05/2012

ISBN: 978-1-4772-1205-9 (sc)

To My
Beautiful
S____ With
Great Love
And
Affection

Volume 1

Volume 1 Contents

A Brief Introduction

The poems and stories in this collection reflect a time in my life when I had finally come out of my cocoon and was ready to feel real love again. Every word in these trifles of my mind are dedicated to the most beautiful woman that I have ever known; my lovely S____. I have spent many years looking for the one woman that would compliment me in every way and would also fit the mould of my favourite words ever spoken in Shakespearean verse; "But till all graces be in one woman, one woman shall not come in my grace" (Much Ado About Nothing Act 2 Scene 3), and in my S____ I have finally found her. These poems represent a new beginning, a new story for me.

S____

If only I could tell you
If only I could say
If only I could reach out and hold you
And let you know I feel this way.

If only my eyes could gaze into yours
If only for a moment we could speak
If only we could meet outside of our lives
Dancing through discovery, cheek to cheek.

If only fanciful thoughts bore reality
If only for a brief and shining moment
If only your hand were interlocked with mine
I would show you the wonders of my heart.

ON THIS WAKEFUL NIGHT

Oh bitter moon . . . how can you so brightly shine
Through my window this eve,
For I am at a loss for words, ensnared by a thought,
A lingering decision, a trap in which I'm caught and can't
escape,
So heavy my heart, longing an embrace where the
Nape of her neck may be a perch for which to lay my
clumsy thoughts.

I see you in my sky, your smile cascading
Through my window, lighting my night from the dark
and dreary,
From the mysterious depths of my cluttered and bereft
Nearly dormant heart, like a beacon through the fog,
An errant arrow from the bow of Eros,
Landing its mark so my mind may find ease.

Oh bitter moon . . . now that you so brightly shine
Through my window and into my heart, help me to pen,
To live, to love through these arts of words and whims,
Help me to softly sing this melody that she has subtly
placed within me,
Her infectious smile, her long black hair, her beautiful
bright brown eyed
Snare that has laid siege to my soul on this wakeful night.

SONG

   . . . now might I confess,
Whisper a dream aloud through a soft caress,
A tender tantric tapestry to weave a spell,
A magic, mystical aura to swoon and swell
   The song that sings in your heart.

I breathe my words like infectious lyric,
Lips and lusts combine as I lose myself
In the contours of your neck, where I linger,
Loitering longingly into your mind, the silent
Breath that escapes your lips, the secret smile
Coyly suppressed, the last thought, eyes closed
On a sleepless night fluttering like a lasting
Dream that copulatively teases open your heart.

   . . . and now might I confess,
Whisper a dream aloud through a soft caress,
A tender tantric tapestry to weave my spell,
So that I may lose myself in the womanly wonders
Of your neck for a while, and find that which
   completes me.

On A Starry Night

On this magical night, bright and clear, star gazing,
At one with the universe, with you,
There has begun a beautiful song in my heart,
A moonlit melody, a waltz of discovery and wonder,
Of hearts on fire, circling, in one-another's orbit.

Through the dense clouds above, on a rainy winter
evening
I plot my course, star chart in hand, heavenly bodies up
above,
Guiding stars aligned with stories to be told,
So that I may always find you, the brightest, the boldest,
The most magnificent star in my sky.

On this magical night, I walk a new path,
A jaunt down love street with my heart on my sleeve,
Meandering here and there,
Plucking philosophical ponderings from the cool night air,
To hold forever in my memory, forever in my soul, in your
world.

On A Cold And Lonely Night

Her soft cheek nestled closer to his chest seeking her spot, rubbing warmly up against his skin, before finally coming to a rest with her brow on the base of his neck. This was her happiest moment of every day, safe, lying in his arms with all of her dreams so firmly within reach. Their union was perfect, one of respect, understanding and kindness. She had finally found someone of like mind, someone with whom to share her life that would not steal her time, and most importantly someone that would let her breath. When she needed him he was there. When she wanted to be alone he understood and stayed away. The more he gave of himself in this way the more she craved him. She was free to explore the world that she wanted to make for herself, she was in love, and she was finding that he was becoming more a part of the world to her.

She opened her eyes and gave a contented sigh. This valentines day may not have been the most romantic, busy work schedules and deadlines to meet, but the memory of their first night, his loving embrace, and the quiet comfort she felt safely nestled into her spot would be all the romance she required for the rest of her life. She closed her eyes and dreamed the beautiful dream of the magical evening when their worlds finally came together. The clear night sky beckoned lovers on this evening. The moon shone brightly overhead as they meandered along the sea-walk and through their pasts; two hearts coming together sharing collective experiences. Even on the most bitter winter night the moon may smile upon lonely hearts. They walked and talked, drawn forward by the breaking dawn, discovering their love for one-another.

He lovingly caressed her brow; every motion performed with heartfelt precision to ease her mind and rest her soul. She was the most beautiful woman he had ever seen. She was precisely everything that he had ever wanted. Her smile was infectious, a magical drug, able to control his every motion and she was always smiling; perpetual sunshine. She was also a firecracker, full of spirit and fire, able to inspire and ignite passion in the coldest of hearts. She was all he could see. Six months of smiles, without words, had passed in the workplace, neither wanting to make that dreaded faux pas. Man made rules dangling like Damocles overhead, waiting to fall. Some rules are meant to be broken no-matter the cost; and she was worth any cost. It was as if he had already made his choice before they ever met, his mind set, waiting for fate to tell him the right moment. On that fateful day the smiles turned into words, the moment had arrived, and love began to blossom on a cold and lonely night.

LOVE KNOWS NO FEAR

How can I ever find the words,
A simplistic, didactic expression
Of nouns, verbs, and turns of phrase
That will allow me to begin to describe my love for you.

I rack my brain in an endless search,
An eloquence of diction,
To break the tongue tied curse that
I feel whenever you are near me.

I open my heart, I bare my soul,
Every word that I write, each syllable,
Rolls through my veins and feeds
my desire for a beautiful discourse with you.

And so I pen my words, and relish my thoughts
Holding tightly to the dream within my heart
To one day express my feelings for you,
And hold you to me, when love knows no fear.

TONIGHT . . .
WITH EMPTY ARMS

I can't chase you from my thoughts,
The sweet sound of your name rolling from my lips,
The smell of your perfume teasing my senses,
Over and over until I close my eyes
And see a perfect picture of you before me,
Your beautiful smile, your soft sideways glances
That quicken the beat of my heart,
And keep me from achieving rest tonight.

I lay awake this night thinking of you,
The clock ticking away into the early morning,
My arms reaching out to a remembered embrace,
Your hands in mine, your head resting upon my shoulder,
Our bodies slowly melding into one,
Discovering each other for the first time, briefly,
And I lay here awake tonight with empty arms
That long to hold you again.

LAPLANTE

Wind dancing candle, your red light flicker has caught
my eye,
The escalating pitch of midnight music resounding in my
mind,
My body shakes, convulsive dreamscape,
Rolling magic fingers keying softly together with the
rhythm,
A violent outburst of passion, a cry of love,
Into the sky above, so far away yet right before me,
Emanating from your soul, encompassing all of us,
Coming to a rest in my heart.

Moonlit Memories

As I lay here, soft moonlight dancing shadows
Across the ceiling, raindrops tapping at my window
In tune with the breaking day, like footsteps
In the sand, pigeon toed in an awkward out of sync step
That always trails to the right
Leading me to the source of my strength,
Where the height of my resolve remains true,
To a magical moment on a clear and starry night,
When love began to blossom between me and you.

I chase the dancing shadow blades, my ceiling fan
spinning my memories back and forth,
in unison with the rain, with the sloshing street traffic
Tumbling toward my towering domain and remember
Walking with you, stride for stride with our
Words as our guide into the evening hours
Slowly stepping our way along the path
Of discovery, sharing our truths and expressing our souls
So that one day we could become you and me.

IF I ONLY KNEW

If I only knew, these four words
Spoken aloud in my own voice, so
Unfamiliar to me in the resounding doubt,
So foreign, have confused the positive
Vibrations that weaken my knees every time
I see your smile, hear your voice
Or dare a glance into your magical eyes.

I race through my mind, chasing thoughts and words,
Trying to remember adjectives, descriptive verbs,
spoken in your sweet, soft celestial voice
that may lead me to a course of action
That I hesitate to pursue, waiting to discover
The missing feeling to unlock these four binding words
That are holding me down, if I only knew.

Shadows In The Night

I watch the shadows dancing across my ceiling,
A plethora of pairs tangoing, step by step in the dark,
Guided only by the pale moonlight as it rises and fades
through windblown trees.
Together they spin, sliding and sashaying
Their way into my mind, moving with the music
that you have implanted in my soul, making me miss you
even more
On this long and lonely evening.

With every second that we're apart my body
Longs for you lying next to me, my hands gently
Caressing your soft back, your slender side,
As your warm and shallow breaths land lovingly
at the base of my neck.
I close my eyes so that I may see your smile,
Be entranced by the magic in your beautiful brown eyes,
and forever be warmed by the love in your heart.

THE SUN IN MY SKY

I am a new man, born again,
Floating freely on the breeze,
My wings spread wide, plumed and plucked
In a playful display,
Teasing and taunting the world around me,
I soar majestically above the clouds
To catch a glimpse of the new sun that has
Appeared in my sky,
So bright, so bold, she shines just for me,
Lighting a new path, a new life,
For I have found that which makes me complete,
My one true love,
My S____.

Missing You

There is an empty space in my bed this evening,
I lie here alone, eyes wide open,
Staring into the cold and empty sheets,
The tediously tidy array of pillows so perfectly plumed,
Feathered and fluffed in mocking comfort.
I force myself to stand, walk three paces to the door,
Turn suddenly, reassess the scene,
Checking for reality with my dumbfounded, tired mind.
I take a clumsy step forward, the emptiness vast before me,
Pushing me back, uninviting me,
What was once comfort and joy is now gone
And I can't rest my thoughts here in this void.
I close my eyes, holding tightly to an image of you
That I carry in my mind, I step forward,
Plunging into the abyss, with thoughts of you, in my
heart,
In my soul, on this lonesome night, missing you.

As One

The skies have opened up, the rain begins to fall,
Heavy drops crashing down upon my upturned brow,
Dampening my face, my neck, but most definitely not my
spirits,
For I am alive in this moment, I have found the real me again,
I am in love, I am connected once more to the endless
Possibilities of this bold and beautiful borderless sky that
covers me,
My warm blanket, my safe haven from a cold and callous,
Uncaring world, my emotional sunshine, star-shine, rain
cloud,
Moonlight majesty, I stand before you in awe, my heart so
full,
Brimming over through uncontrollable smiles for all to
see, my arms
Spread wide so that I may embrace your vast and glorious
wonders,
Your salacious sermons so sweetly showering upon me one
drop at a time
In an endless dance, I spin freely to the music in the air,
Windblown tree top tango, wave swept ocean waltz's
drowning the dizzying
Droning of the white line traffic thunder, so far away from
my mind,
I am free when I am with you, my heart beating in time
with your song,
The light and the dark together as one before me,
As if for the first time, for the last time, for all time,
we are connected, never to be apart.

How Can I . . .

Oh . . . how can I express this feeling that
Has caught hold of me, this wondrous,
Warm rush that has come over me, the soul shaking
Shudder that I feel when you run your fingers
Across my back, my neck, my outstretched arm
That beckons you to come closer every moment
That we're apart?

How can I put into words, how can I pen
The excitement that I feel when you are near me,
The overwhelming urge to pull you close to me,
To cover you with my warm embrace,
Our bodies tightly tied together,
Becoming one, closer and closer,
Unified, you and me?

Oh dear me . . . how can I express this amazing
Feeling that has taken over me, every thought I have,
Every beat of my heart, they are all for you my one and
only,
My sexy, sultry, sensory overloading love of my life,
My beautiful brown eyed flower, my amazing angel?
I love you with every fibre of my being,
And I always will.

THE BEAUTIFUL GIFT

Tonight,
with rain soaked steps,
I walk my way back home,
Through sloshing streets I stride,
The wind at my back, my head held high to the dripping
clouds,
Catching every precious drop, absorbing the power and
the strength
Of this beautiful gift, this driving force that regenerates us all,
The source of all things living, alight before my eyes,
enveloping me,
Teaching me, teasing and tempting me to quicken my pace,
To flee from this magical walk, to seek shelter
From emotional waterfalls, cold cascading teardrops
imploring me
To understand, to give myself to a union of perfect bliss,
To glide in heavenly strides through these dampened
downtown
Streets and catch a glimpse of true love,
So I slow my steps, accepting the invitation,
For on this eve with cloudy skies, moistened tear stained
eyes,
There is a gentle song that can be heard, a far away
Faint woodwind melody that plays only for me,
Enticing me to dance, to swing and sway, to raise my arms
To the sky and lead the way into a brighter tomorrow,
To carry this tranquil tune to others,
And spread this feeling of love.

A Second Chance At Love

I am overwhelmed, taken aback, humbled,
And shaken to the core by this wonderful, colourful
And crazy gift that has been bestowed upon me.

So many nights, lying alone in my bed
Did I imagine a plethora of possibilities, a dreamers dream of
Second chances, forbidden secret romances that
Would lift my heart from despair.

An endless array of musings, trapped inside my muddy
Misbegotten mind waiting to escape from fantastic
thought
And become the budding fruits of reality.

And so I sat so patiently, waiting and wanting,
Flexing and flaunting my avaricious aria's of pen and paper
So that one day I could set forth on this journey,
This magical caper to steal your heart.

Now . . . here we stand, two lovers lost in a land of
Late night kisses, lingering and loitering a little longer
Through these delicious moments locked tightly to
One-another, two bodies, two hearts,
One burning desire living a lament created up above,
Just in time, forever to be told as these tales of romance go,
As a second chance at love.

Dedicated To You

There is a new song that resonates within my soul,
A timeless tune that keys so sweetly
With my every thought,
That makes me want to dance, that makes me want to
sing,
Makes me see the sunshine in everything around me,
So that I can't contain my love,
So that I write my words and shout your name
From the top of the highest peak,
To tell the world, my beautiful S____,
That my heart is yours to keep,
And I am forever, dedicated to you.

THIS AMOROUS DREAM

The soft, sweet song of your voice
Echo's through my mind tonight,
Carrying me gently to a soothing slumber where the
Warmth of your sunny smile sends me spinning
Deeper and deeper into this supine state,
This amorous dream where your beautiful disposition
Coddles me in an all encompassing bath,
Where your touch sends tingles down my spine,
Raises heaven in my heart,
And brings peace and quiet to my frantic,
Frenetic, felicitous thoughts.

Our Secret Love

I stand alone, remove myself from your sumptuous side,
Watch your emotions from a distance,
And hold tightly to the love that I feel for you.

Our secret love, it seems impossible to contain,
To hold back from putting my arms around you,
From kissing your soft and sensuous lips,
But we force ourselves apart.

I feel a weight in the pit of my stomach,
An ache that bends me in half, tears at my very soul,
And burns a hole in my heart every second
I'm near you, yet so far away.

I can't stand to live this way, to be your love
And pretend that we're not together,
To contain these feelings that burn so brightly between us,
Seems an agony that I can't bear.

I want to kiss you, I want to hold you,
I want to run my fingers through your hair
And embrace the bold and brash sentiments
That have moulded us together and helped to
Create our perfect love.

MY BEAUTIFUL S ____

I wish I had the words to describe this feeling,
An expression that could accurately articulate the warmth,
The perpetual glow that emanates from your eyes
And lights my way when I am lost beneath the dark
deceptive clouds,
The rusty ruinous skies that rise from time to time,
And attempt to hold me down, to pin me to the ground
and diffuse
The melody that meanders through my mind,
The magical music that you sing to me with each glorious
glance,
The symphonic stares on rainy Saturday mornings, lying
in bed together,
Wrapped tightly to one-another, arms and legs fusing
In a twisted, tepid embrace,
My burning desire for you growing hotter with each
passing moment,
A cumulative, copulative, charismatic crescendo bursting
forth
So bright that our love has bloomed and blossomed like a
twice lit candle, a star in the night guiding me toward my
fatalistic future, to the world I was meant to see,
To feel, to describe in ink and words,
A wonderful wisdom that I embrace every moment that I am
Basking in your beauty, cradled in your arms, and lost in
your eyes.

Sunday Sunset

The sun slowly sets, I sit here on this bench,
Staring out over the horizon, the beach,
The bitter cold wind that bites my cheeks,
The crashing waves riding high on the rocks,
Sweeping the sediment and sand, swiftly surrounding my feet,
Tying my toes to this transcendental thought that
Hangs heavy in my mind, my longing lament
That springs forth from my pursed lips as I
Kiss the sky on this whimsical evening in which I find
Myself pondering futures and fates,
Elastic elemental states of being that I keep
Bouncing through on my journey in this tormented,
Tremendous, tedious, ticklish, tasteless,
Timeless rollercoaster ride of limericks and love,
This mystical, mysterious marvel that we call life.

CELESTIAL SIGNS

This lonely night, with eyes wide open
I lay here staring into space
Searching the stars for a celestial sign,
A heavenly body that sweetly slips
Into my arms warming my heart and soul.

How I long for your touch,
A gentle caress along my spine
Your tickling fingers across my neck
That seek and slide through my hair
And quiet my restless mind.

This lonely night, with eyes wide open
I hold tightly to my dreams of you
The promise of a beautiful future,
Where every night I hold you in my arms
And every morning I wake to your amazing smile.

WHERE I LIVE NOW

Everyday, in every way, I am amazed by you,
Awestruck by your elegance, enlightened by
Your enigmatic, elusive manner that keeps
Me guessing, keeps me confessing my fastidious
Feelings, my secret wants, eccentric flaunts,
That set me apart from the rest of the pack.

I stand aside, walk alone, apart from the
World with my own steadfast stride,
Along a narrow path, a trail less tried,
Traversing time and space, through intangible thoughts
And theory's, cosmic questioning queries,
That have magically landed me in your grace
Where I live now in your sensual splendour.

THIS SWEET DREAM

When I wake from this magical slumber,
Stolen from this sweet dream back into
This cold and empty bed where I lay alone
Without your warm and wonderful body next to me,
I will turn my thoughts to the satisfying
Serenity of your voice, your siren song sung
So sweetly, your sumptuous sensory stealing lips,
Locking lovingly to mine, longing to linger
A little while longer in this tender embrace.

With eyes closed tightly, I stretch my hand
To slide along your slender side, slinking softly
To touch your spine, tickling and teasing you,
Tempting a torrid kiss, connecting our bodies
In a tangled bliss filled tapestry of love struck limbs,
Sewn together through soft sentimental wishes
That have come to pass between us, connecting our
Hearts and minds, binding our lives tonight on this
Intertwined journey through this sweet dream.

WITH EVERY BREATH
(YOU FILL ME)

I stare into the face of the evening sky,
So lonely this night, the street lights
Revealing the pathway to another world,
A future so near at hand, yet elusive,
Impossible to grasp at this time, in this place,
Far across the water, you lay peacefully in slumber,
Your beautiful form, so soft and supple,
A glimmer in the moonlight, a magical,
Mystical memory of our nights together,
that keeps me strong when we're apart.

I feel you within me with every beat of my heart,
Your lovely skin, a mnemonic sensation
In my fingertips when I sense you near me,
Yet so far from my touch,
With every breath you fill me with a world of wonders,
For you are the sun in my sky,
The light that guides me on my way
Toward a better tomorrow, a dream in which
I long to live, hand in hand, heart to heart,
With the woman that I love, for the rest of my life.

Volume 2

VOLUME 2 CONTENTS

AN INTRODUCTION
TO VOLUME 2

This second volume of poems is a continuous journey through the lives of two people that somehow found each other. Our love continues to grow daily beneath a shroud of secrecy. One day these words will live freely amongst the poetics of others in the free world where musings and meandering thoughts of this nature may inspire true love to blossom against all odds. As stated in the volume 1 introduction the poems contained in this collection are dedicated to the most beautiful woman that I have ever known, my beautiful and amazing S____.

EIGHT LITTLE LETTERS
(FOREVER IN MY MIND)

Do you remember?

The words of love, a simple expression,
The triumphant trident that pierced my heart,
drew open the imprisoning doors of the past and bridged
imaginary gaps
Between us, eight little letters so softly spoken,
A sentimental dream lying together under moonlit skies,
Shadowed tree dancing spirits before our eyes
Across my bedroom ceiling.

Do you remember?

That wonderful day we spent together,
The first of many, hand in hand with the sun
Cascading it's warmth upon our shoulders,
Revealing a silhouetted glimpse of the road ahead,
Two lovers caught up in a trance within each other's eyes,
A secret celebratory dance that will
Forever echo through my mind.

Do you remember?

These moments of our beginning,
A blossoming love on the eve of your birth,
when a connection was made as your lips
Landed on my cheek, and my resolve to be with you
Once seemingly beyond my reach
Had fallen into my grasp as I held you to me
For the first time, with our first night,
And our first kiss, forever in my mind.

Right Where I Belong

Tonight, I feel a sensation deep inside,
A splendid sensory surge that sends shivers
Along my skin in goose bumped decorum,
Teasing a timeless smile upon my face and in my spirit,
A loving, liberated laughter that has longed for
Release for so many nights that it has brimmed over
Me with every slight touch of your hands,
Your lips, your body pressed close to mine,
I am sated, revelling in a raucous irreverent display
Of feverish delight.

I hold you to me, bodies uniting, warm and tender,
Our embrace a searching and soulful blending of
Surging synapses echoing savagely to break
The silence of the evening, a torrid tale of tender
Touches traversing the length and breadth of your
Tantalizing torso, caressing and clawing a circuitous,
Copulative course along your shoulders to your spine,
Every moment my lips lingering a moment longer
Along your lavish neck, your ear lobes,
Lost in salivary, seductive loving kisses that seem
To last all night.

Tonight, my deepest inner thoughts and feelings
Are forever etched upon my skin,
A crazy compilation of curiosity and comfort
That has been uncovered by your soft caress,
Your loving nature and your sweet and soulful smile
That every day, in every way brings out the best in me,
For you are the source of all my strength,
The smile within my soul that moves me to write
These words, create new songs, to live and to love
Out loud for the world to see, right where I belong.

Our Beautiful Secret

I watch the seconds tick away, in a maddening,
Frustrating, malicious melody, rolling slowly into
Minutes and hours that only extend this malady that
I feel when you are away from me, and so . . .
I reminisce with my memories of our moments together,
The sensation of our slightly parted lips,
A fusion of warm breaths escaping slowly between soft,
Searching kisses where our hearts meet briefly in a
Closed eye vision of our love for each other.

I close my eyes now so that I may escape this time
And place, clutching tightly to your pillow so that
I may transport myself into your embrace through
The scent of your sweet perfume,
Your lovely body impressed before me in the sheets,
the last lingering remnant of our beautiful secret love
that I hold so near and dear to my heart, on this night
where though our bodies lay separately, miles apart,
I know that our souls are always going to be connected.

WHEN TIME STANDS STILL

I am fleet of foot this evening,
Well rested and awake, giddy with the thought
That I may spend a few minutes in your presence,
And so I jump from rock to rock in and endless dance,
Skipping lightly to the pending moments
When our romance resumes on this
Clandestine bus ride to your home.

With the anticipation of your smile,
your beautiful eyes upon me,
Your hand grasping tightly to mine,
I revel at the prospects and the possibilities
Of all our tender you and me eccentricities
Occurring in this magical moment when though our
Earthbound bodies are in transit, our hearts
And minds are removed from time to bask in the
Thrill of this moonlit ride when time stands still
And we are finally alone together.

Tonight, And Every Night

Where do I begin?, so many muddled thoughts,
Secret strands, forget me not's, spinning endlessly
within my brain causing a crippling plethora of sleepless
nights
In which I drag my troubled, turbulent, temperament
Back and forth over imaginary coals in an endless circle
until I can articulate appropriately, with an accurate
acumen,
The complex poetic choreography, that will allow me to be
understood.

Tonight, with triumphant resonance, I have resolved
These tumultuous theoretical tangents, traversed this
Terrible trap to find myself tied tightly by my heart-strings
To the woman of my dreams, so perfect in every way,
Always there for me, unafraid of the words that others
Dare not say, and forever surprising me with her
Beautiful caring ways.

And now I need not ask where it is that I may begin?,
The truth laid out before me written in ink, spoken
In soft voices late at night through a telephonic exchange,
Laying together in a dream where my simple, secret,
Sensational thoughts, may be shared with you as I
Speak softly upon your neck and save my tortured
Soul one syllable at a time.

My beautiful S_____, you are my saving grace,
My sanity restoring, amazing angel faced love,
I hold you to me every moment of every day,
Planning for a future not too far away in which we
Will grow and share together, our secret love blossoming
Every day until it may no-longer be contained and
The outside world will stand in awe of what we've become.

And so . . . tonight, I pledge to you my words
And my heart, forever and always to tell you
From the very start that which runs through my mind,
Runs through my soul, to keep you apprised of all that
Is me, all that is you within me, and our wonderful life
That we build stronger each and every day, as we walk
Hand in hand, heart to heart, toward the future, together.

Basking In Your Light

My confident stride has escalated this sunny day,
A spring in my step, a skip added here and there
Emanating from the words of love that you have just
Shared with me, my smile brighter than the afternoon sky
For you have filled me with joy by speaking three little words,
Holding my hand, and looking up at me with those
magical
Brown eyes that always warm my heart.

I move swiftly through the streets, a song in my soul
Slowly seeping through every pore, a sweet soliloquy
That slips through my lips and into the air around me,
Carrying high up over the trees, circling me in an all
encompassing
Breeze that directs me homeward toward the bright
And better future that I see every time
You and I engage in a kiss.

Your love is all around me, surrounding me like a
Warm blanket, a solid embrace that holds me high above the
Daily grind of this work-a-day world and stations me
Steadfast in your bountiful light, beaming brightly
From your lovely smile, your beautiful aura
Lighting my life so that no-matter how stressful my day
One secret sideways glance from you and I'm floating
High above the clouds in love with the world that has
Given me the amazing gift of spending my life with you.

Our Warm Embrace

I can't sleep this night, my bed so empty,
Barren and cold, once warm only one evening ago
With my beautiful lady, her lovely body pressed
Tightly to mine, melding her to me, arms and legs
Tied together in a lovers embrace, upside down in bed,
The moonlight dancing across your sleeping face,
So peaceful, your lips inviting a kiss, the nape of your neck
Bare before me beneath my cheek, so tempting, your tasty
Skin I long to touch as our hearts beat in unison,
Breathing one breath, knowing peace and quiet, living a
lifetime
Of love in this cherished moment.

I whisper wanting words to you in your sleep,
Revealing my secret dreams, my hidden heartfelt
Helpless feelings told only for you, my beautiful angel,
My sweet S____, I run my hand along your spine,
Teasing and tickling, your goose bumped flesh talking to
me
In body brail messages, I read every inch of your skin
and know that you love me, our warm embrace a story
that we
Live to share each and every night, always and forever,
A promise to pass on to the generations to follow
As you smile sweetly in response to my query,
And I am able to quiet my thoughts, and fall asleep.

Bound Together

This morning, far from the warmth of your
Slender figure, I woke alone, away from
Our Saturday morning bed where we playfully
Paw at one-another with longing looks,
Lip-locked love-making moments and
Tender embraces where whispered secret thoughts
Are shared between us, as this morning,
For the first time, you and I were apart on this day,
And I awoke feeling lost and without comfort.

Last night, through modern miracles of convenience,
We spoke in muted tones as you lay quietly in your bed
And I upon my couch, so far apart,
Yet still close enough for our words to find solace,
As if we were locked together,
You within my arms, perfectly placed,
Moulded in this embrace,
A matched pair that were meant to find each other
And live their lives as one.

This evening, I lay on my couch again, wanting your
touch,
Searching the rainy skies for a glimpse of your heavenly
smile,
Your luscious lyrical love songs hummed in my ear,
My eyes shut tight to the cold world around us,
With only the warmth of our bodies our love may burn
For a thousand lifetimes, and we, so daring,
Fan the flames further with caring words and cumulative
kisses,

That when added together would create a number
Beyond reckoning, and our lips still burn for more.

I wait for the next night that we may be together,
I lay here, holding your hand tightly to my chest
Though it is not within my grasp, my phantom touch
Upon your back as you lay sleeping,
Our bodies brought together through words of love
Late at night, as we lay apart, my love for you,
Stronger than any distance between us, shall reach out to you
Always and forever, for we are meant to be, a pair from
one mould,
Bound by love, I will always find you,
For I am a part of you, and you are the best part of me.

MY DEAR S____
(CLOSE YOUR EYES)

Close your eyes my love
And listen to my words
For though I speak to you from afar
They will bring us closer together.

Do not be afraid my dear
The shadows of the night
And the ghosts of days gone by
Shall not break the bond that we have formed together.

Close your eyes my love
And listen to the beating of my heart
For though you are not within my arms tonight
It beats solely for you and you alone.

Do not despair my dear
These days that we're apart
The solitary nights will not last much longer
And we will soon share our dreams again upon the same
pillow.

So close your eyes my love
And let my words paint you a picture
A dream of days alone together
Walking sandy beaches hand in hand.

Do not worry my dear
For I will always be here for you
Our love shall carry us to the life in our dreams
Where happiness awaits for you and me.

A Beautiful Portrait

Goodnight my love,
Close your eyes and fall asleep
Let your troubles drift away,
For I am with you tonight,
You and I cheek to cheek in slumber,
Two hearts beating as one, our bodies united,
A beautiful portrait,
A physical manifestation of the multitude
Of I love you's so softly spoken between us.

Goodnight my love,
Close your eyes and dream your dreams
For you are safe tonight within my arms,
Your home away from home,
Where you are always welcome,
My heart craving the warmth of your body,
The softness of your skin,
The secret smiles we share in public etched
On your face once again as we lay here,
Together, reminiscing the journey of our secret love.

Goodnight my love,
Close your eyes and hold me tight
For I am in need of your embrace,
It has been too long since the last time,
I hold you now, and I can't wait until the next
Night that we may be alone together,
The love rush adrenal anticipation keeping me awake,
So darling please, squeeze my hand and pull me to you,

Our bodies united so that I may live
My favourite dream in this moment, such a beautiful
portrait,
and fall asleep in this loving pose with you.

You Quiet My Mind

Tonight, my heart alight with passion,
I hold you in my arms as you lay sleeping,
And I know deep down inside,
The butterflies churning in my stomach,
That my life, in all of its forms, the pleasure and the pain,
From day to day, revolves around my desire
To be with you, to hold you, to love you,
For you are the music in the air beckoning me to sing,
To write my words, dance to the joy of the musings
That you place in my heart by merely being
Near you.

I awake, to the thunderous rain,
The windblown trees slapping feverishly at my window,
Your shallow breaths warm against my hand
Grasping tightly to you, lovingly I stroke your hair
As I thank you for being here with me,
My mind racing to find the happiness that the
Violent storm outside has robbed from me,
And you turn to me, your beautiful brown eyes
Searching my face, and you knowingly kiss my brow
With your soft lips and whisper words of love in my ear,
The pale blue glow of the moonlight illuminating our
Tender embrace as you quiet my mind and pull
Me toward you, cradle me in your arms,
And I fall back asleep, my happiness restored,
even more in love with you.

In Any Language

Je t'aime mon bebe,
The words ring true within my head,
Within my heart, and slide so sweetly
From my tongue that they must sound just
As beautiful to anyone else, truer words,
They have never been spoken aloud,
For I am so in love with you that every
Moment apart my chest pains every time your
Name rolls through my thoughts,
Every second of every day.

Ik hou van je mijn baby,
My pen writes every little secret word
That you have taught me, your love so bright
That my eyes struggle to see without you near me
For the world away from you is dark and dreary,
The flowers no longer bloom, the morning bird songs
muted,
I walk, a stoic figure, through black and white
Streets where the sun is not willing to shine
Until my beautiful S____ may light my sky
Once more.

I love you my baby,
I sing these wonderful words out loud
On a daily basis, the meaning so profound
To me, so magical within my heart and soul,
An all encompassing light that surrounds me,
My perpetual glow that illuminates
My poetic parables, my stylus in hand,

Ever-ready to reunite with ink and paper
In a bond that in any language shall illustrate
That the blood that flows through my veins
It flows for you, true blue, my love.

Falling (In Love)

I have fallen,
I plunge deeper every second
With every searching kiss, your breath, my breath,
Flesh gently touching flesh, not yet locked my lips seeking
yours,
We tempt and we tease, tonguing the edges and corners
To weaken our knees so that we may take this trip together
through
Tantric bliss, as we finally find the moment to merge,
Eyes closed to the world, there's no need to see what we
can't miss,
What we know by touch, memory, instinct, the
temperature rising,
Our love and our lust combining for a moment of pure
unbridled pleasure.

I have fallen,
I give in to this feeling every time,
A backward free fall where I drop my inhibitions
And saturate myself in the moment, a salivary celebration,
So sumptuous one could swear that celestial synergy had
bore the idea,
This thought of you and me together here and now,
the heat between us, the energy, enough to power the stars,
we twist our tongues together in a torrential torrid
downpour
Of tasty temptations,
And we've only just kissed.

I have fallen,

I drop further and further with every rhyme
That floats from my mind and escapes on my breath,
Every word that touches your soul I relive
With unquenchable gestures of the heart,
Our bodies aflame with a burning desire to live each
moment as if it were our last,
We devour each other with clawing nails and nibbling bites,
A pleasurable platitude of earthly delights as we cling to
the strings of
One-another's hearts and pick a tune so soothing that
We've no choice but to fall head over heels in love.

Do I Dare?

I face this new day sun with slight trepidation,
A small insignificant fear in the back of my mind,
A nagging noise that rattles and rings like static feedback,
Never moving forward, regression ever present in its
Annoying tune, ad-nauseoum, over and over yet never over,
Knawing at me from within, this rotting stench that I
despise,
Loath, and still languish over from time to time.

I have finally found this new day sun,
So bright and beautiful before my eyes,
A soft glow that shapes the possibilities of tomorrow
Into perfect little pictures, framed and fixed in fanciful
facets
That my imagination had long since conjured and longed
for,
Now so prevalent, within my weary grasp for the first time
in a long time,
So close to my heart that I dare not grab hold for fear,
though I long to.

I stand before this new day sun, basking in your amazing
light,
And know with every fibre of my body and soul,
That I have never been here before, that this time
everything is different,
Your warmth does not just emanate from without, but
from within,
Flowing through my veins, a river of love overflowing,
engulfing me

And all that I am, slowly quieting and allaying my fears,
Allowing me the ability to breathe life once again.

And so I stand before my new day sun full of hope,
Dreams of tomorrow painted prominently before my eyes,
Dripping water colour skies, pastel promenades that coat
and cover
My barefoot wayward walking, dancing sideways, spinning
feet,
With my perfect pictured future, hand in hand,
My love stalwartly affixed by my side,
Everyday, everywhere I may go.

And so we stand together, my new day sun and I,
Lighting the world with our youthful exuberant love,
A decadent delight that we have captured hand in hand,
Cheek to cheek, in our secret moments where thoughts
and fears
Fall aside to the power and the glory of our passions for
one-another,
And I know in this moment, and believe with all of my
heart,
That my tiny insignificant fear need never return,
My questions in this life, answered by her smile every
time,
And the future within my palm, and so little nagging fear
before you
Depart me forever you ask of me do I dare?

Yes I do!

Heart And Soul

I have found that which has been missing,
The final piece of the puzzle,
The sun in my sky that brightens my day
every time I see her face,
My beautiful flower that blooms and blossoms
Quickening the pace of my heart,
For she is all that I have ever wanted,
My every desire all rolled into one magnificent little lady,
So graceful, so elegant,
My heart and soul, I have finally found you,
And now I'm complete.

Always And Forever

Good morning my beautiful,
How was your sleep last night?,
Did my whispered words of love send you to
A magical dreamland?, a white sand wonder
Where we walk together, our bare feet
Warmed by every wave of the tropical tides,
The soothing breezes and seductive sun splashed palm
trees
Swaying to the rhythm of the music in our hearts,
The tenderness in our touch, and the passion in our eyes.

Did my arms wrap around you in your sleep as
They did here in this bed?,
Where our bodies lay together,
My hands interlocked in yours, pressed tightly to your
breast,
Our feet entangled, hips held close,
My warm breath upon your neck where I whisper
My nurturing words to quiet your mind,
So that you may sleep and dream our beautiful
Dream, with me, always and forever.

THESE NIGHTS OF SOLITUDE

On nights like these, alone and missing you,
I turn to the sanctuary of the words that encapsulate our
love,
Our collected days painted in poetry, an articulate attempt
To recreate the wondrous emotions that you stir in me,
The commitment that I hold so near and dear to my
heart,
My ever growing love for you so vast
And overwhelming that it pains me when
You are beyond my reach, my sight.

On these nights alone, it is as though
The world has grown colder, quiet,
Empty of all that I cherish, a solitude too much to bear,
Like a great weight placed upon my chest,
Pinning me to this lonely feeling without the warmth of
you touch,
The magic of your smile, the air stolen from me so that I
must
Fight to breathe until I am once again alleviated by the
awesome,
All encompassing spark of life that fills my lungs,
And energizes my heart, my S____, I love you.

IN THIS WORLD
(ONLY YOU AND ME)

When this dream ends I will open my eyes,
Find my arms empty, laying alone in this empty bed,
This empty room of little comfort to the storm outside,
As I step into the early hours the cold wind shall blow
A harsh reminder through these darkened hours,
I will hunch my shoulders for warmth and walk a
quickened pace,
My head down, the moon fading slowly from the sky
As the new day begins to break,
But for now I will shut tight my already opening eyes,
And remain in this lavish setting, holding tightly
To this magical dream world where I can be with you,
At the least, for the remainder of this night.

The wonder of our softly spoken words washes over me,
Pillow talk dreams of days to come where the tide is high,
The wave swept beach glistens white beneath the days sun,
Crashing warm ripples upon the sand, the ocean's majesty
Erasing our coupled footsteps behind us as we saunter
hand in hand,
The soothing breeze at our backs cooling our necks,
Playfully sweeping your hair from right to left across your face,
You turn toward me, your barefoot stance,
Entrenched in softened sediment, you light up my life,
Your beautiful smile my umbrella under cloudy skies,
We embrace, your head against my chest, and
There is only you and me in this world.

We set our feet, sand seeping between toes,
Share a silly smile and speed off down the shore,
Fingertips reaching to maintain their grip while we
Run along the surf, the wind swept waves crashing all around
Our fumbling footsteps, a water dancing whirlwind
Splashing between us as we tumble to the ground,
Rolling to a stop side by side, our arms immediately
searching,
Grasping to one-another, we slide tenderly together,
Your wave wet hair between my fingers as my eyes search your
Eyes, our lips whispering warm air kisses,
Our brows meet for a moment, nuzzling noses
Sliding side by side, we roll toward the setting sun
And marvel at the magic of this life we've made together.

As this amorous dream comes to its end, I force my eyes
To remain shut for a moment longer, my mind searching,
Not yet satisfied, needing to know the end result of this
Beautiful scene, the why's and the where's,
Locations unknown too far from here where the cold wind
Blazes reality back into my sleepy soul, I strive to see the
end of this scene,
The setting sun, the hazy beach with you and me lying
together in the sand,
walking up from the water's edge toward our beautiful
beach front home,
And I am satisfied to open my eyes, the dark gloom
Of this rainy day no-longer in my sight, the wind
Not so cold anymore, I walk to work tall and proud
With the future sun blazing brightly over my shoulders.

THIS GIFT (IN MY SOUL)

I can hear it in your voice, in your late night
Early morning whispers, like a soft echo within my head,
The flutter in my heart that ignites my desire,
and spurs me on to write my words and sing my songs,
To see and feel the beauty that is all around me
With a brand new set of eyes, as though I've been born
again,
Eager and ready to experience this roller coaster ride
That we call life, and I know deep down inside,
That you're the one.

I can see it in your smile, your luscious lips that I
Long to kiss, your eyes alight, dancing left and right
With unfettered joy and happiness whenever I am in your
sight,
And I am filled with hope, ready for the possibilities of
each new day,
Standing tall, standing proud, waiting to embrace every
challenge
That comes my way with a smile on my face,
A song in my heart, a picture of you that I carry in my
mind,
My every thought bound to you, my one and only love,
For I know, that you are the one.

I can feel it in your touch, your slender fingers sliding
Gently between mine, grasping tightly, hand in hand,
We walk together through this life, this gift that we've
been given,
The sweet and sensual tickle across my spine,

The gentle caress of my brow as you tussle my hair,
I close my eyes and feel your energy inside of me,
You are in my soul, our spirits dancing, having found each
other,
And complete am I for the first time in my life,
With my girl by my side, because, you are the one.

THESE NIGHTS
WITHOUT MY LOVE

There is a bitter staleness in the air tonight,
As though I've been here before, breathed this dirty air
already,
And now recognize the foulness of this repetition,
This hateful night where I stand alone in a crowd of
strangers,
Pretending that I want to be here, that everything is ok,
Lying through clenched teeth and tired eyes,
Longing to be free from this burden, to be back where I
belong,
Back in the arms of my lovely lady of whom I miss so
much
That it pains me to close my eyes, for she resides in my
every thought,
My lungs aching to call out, her name on the tip of my
tongue
Waiting to drip from my mouth in a never-ending
waterfall of wanton words,
A rhyming rhetoric filled with my eccentricities and
playful verve
That will express my pure and true love through poetic
pleasantries
That I carry in my heart each and every day,
My endless passion for this perfect woman that I have
somehow found,
And I treasure her with every fibre of my being,

My one true love, my soul mate, my S____,
I write to you this evening with tears welling up in my
eyes,
And the heaviest of hearts because I miss you so much
That I can barely breathe, and so I scramble to find
something to distract me,
A momentary escape from this unbearable anguish,
As a new day breaks before me I stare out at the rising sun,
Another day without you, and I look to the sky above,
I close my eyes, clinging tightly to the picture of you that I
carry in my mind
Though it pains me to do so, and I attempt to find the
strength
To make it through another of these lonely nights without
my love.

It Is You

It is you my love, my first thought every morning,
My last thought every night, my beautiful flower whose
Bloomed blossom perfume sets my soul on fire,
And whose colourful petals ensnare my senses,
My thoughts, my sights set solely on you.

It is you my lady, with your beautiful brown eyes
beaming with delight, your hair cascading down your
back,
your soft satin skin, the contours of your neck,
That trap and tantalize me,
So that I might take my time to touch you so softly.

It is you my S____, that has laid siege to my heart,
And set me on this flight of fancy,
For every smile, every word, every little move,
Makes me love you only that much more,
And so now my one desire, I shall spend each day,
For the rest of my life, loving you with all that I am,
For it is you my dear, that one day in the future,
I will ask to be my wife.

THIS MOMENT OF PERFECTION

. . . may I live my life forever within this single moment,
This blissful beginning, forever in my mind,
Always around me no-matter where I may go,
This amazing feeling will always allow me the strength,
The audacity, and the ability to accomplish anything.

I am in awe, inspired by your words, your kind heart,
Your beautiful smile, the way that you look at me,
The fire in your eyes, your all encompassing love,
Like a warm blanket, wrapped around me,
My protection from the cold,
The source of my strength and the smile in my soul.

With each new day, rain or shine, you are the sun in my
sky,
The brightest star to light up the night, perpetually
glowing,
Always bright, showing me the road ahead,
My future so close at hand for the first time,
And so . . . may I live my life forever within this single
moment,
Where everyday I may feel just as I felt with you in my
arms,
on our first night, when I fell in love with you,
For the rest of my life.

In Your Eyes

I was lost, adrift in a sea of despair,
Longing for home, a warm embrace in which
I could find refuge from the storm, the endless
Barrage of emotional tides that have tried to pull me
under,
Ripping and tearing at me, until I found you.

I was lost, my wayward walking shoes refusing
To kick up the dust of the road less traveled,
Stuck in the mud, the unkempt remains of the past,
Surrounding and stifling, dragging me under,
Losing my lustre, until one glorious day when I found
you.

I was lost, and then you saved me with a smile,
Playful and mischievous, the truth in your eyes,
Ready to tell me everything about you with a single
glance,
The magic and the mystery, your ever present passion,
Inspiring the promise in me that I'll never look away.

I was lost for a time, until I found myself in your eyes,
Where I want to remain for the rest of my life,
Finally home, never to be alone,
For this fire between us burns eternal, my love for you,
An exponential envelopment, our bodies, our hearts,
Our souls fused together as one, forever,
Now that we've found each other.

LULLABY

Close your eyes my dear, empty your mind
Of all your troubling thoughts, and listen to my words,
Let them take you away, your body laying still in your bed,
Totally at ease, feel my hands in your hands,
My feet, hips, knees, together with yours,
Our bodies tied tightly, you are safe,
My arms wrapped around you in our warm embrace,
My lips gently kissing your neck, our hearts beating in
unison,
A beautiful rhythm, a lullaby of love to sing you to sleep
On nights that we are apart my precious S____.

. . . so close your eyes my dear, empty your mind of
Of all your troubling thoughts, and let my words take you
Away from here to a place where we are together,
Where our love is free, set loose upon the world for all to see
How you light up my life with the magic in your eyes,
How your smile sets my soul on fire, burning brighter
every day,
My lovely lady, hear my words, close your eyes and go to
sleep,
For I will always be here, my arms wrapped tightly around you,
My lips kissing your neck, our hearts beating together,
Emanating our beautiful love, our rhythmic lullaby.

Our Time Together

Counting time, like backward steps through the snow,
Retracing, three, two, one, back to the quay where it all
started,
With the sun shining brightly over our shoulders,
Shades of the future being cast before us,
The magical day that I fell in love with you,
Not so long ago, yet still so far in the past.

How do we begin to measure time?, adding the hours,
The minutes, all of these numbers do not compare
To the emotions in our words and in our touch,
Mere moments that last a lifetime in my mind,
That mean so much when all is said and done,
Not so long ago, yet still so far in the past.

In our time together, though short, we have loved
A lifetimes worth, my heart still burning for you
As bright as it did that first night out on the beach,
Under a starry sky on a cold and lonely night when
Two lovers began to unite and fall in love,
And here we stand, two months later, a measure of time,
Yet so much more between us in our time together,
Not so long ago, and still so much farther to go.

MUSIC OF THE HEART

The glistening raindrops cascaded from the sky in a luminescent sheet, projected through early morning street lights, making the street look like a scene from an old movie. With rain dampened hair matted to his forehead, his spirit alight with the thought of this evenings events still fresh in his mind, he walked home past the beach with a smile on his face. The waves rolling in over the sand, stirring up emotions long since forgotten, pleasurable upon their return, loosened from the sediment of the past, lightened his steps. Their first night together was a magical walk amongst the stars only one week prior to tonight, but this evening was different. This evening was the one that would change everything forever, for it was certain in his mind, this was love. There was still the faint echo of music in the air from earlier at the jazz club; music that his ears would forever remember in connection with her amazing smile. All of his senses were alive. She was the one.

The solo saxophone filled the empty spaces in the open room with heartfelt emotion; pouring forth from every aspect of the man's being. The artist spitting his fire from his soul to the gasping, teeth clenched, hush amongst the scattered few in attendance. At the close of the performance his body, as if being held up by his passion, collapsed upon the stage like a pile of discarded clothing. He had ripped through the woodwind instrument like a tropical storm. The room had transformed, the candle lit red glow beckoning the wind to blow again, into a beautiful moment from the transcendent past of jazz folklore. Matthias looked around the room, surveying the post modern jazz scene of the boastful Vancouver press releases, and scoffed at the crowd that had formed on this evening. The ragtag audience consisted of : well to-do gas-town baby-boomer couples of the chit chat, wine guzzling, searching for the next witty and urbane water cooler conversation to boast about at the next soiree ilk; local gas-town hipsters feeling the need to perpetuate a pastiche approach to life that would eventually culminate in the miscreant college casserole of everything in the cupboard that they had lived only a few years earlier; and then there were the two lovers out on their second date looking to find a connection with one-another through the beautiful music in the air. He rolled his eyes at the depths of depravity, the pretentious air looming heavy around them, and wished to go back in time to when this type of music belonged to real people. When music meant something. When hearts and minds were stirred by the passion in the air and falling in love was always on the menu. When blues and jazz clubs were located in areas much like this, only not transformed into upscale urban chic retrofit suites where those with too much money and too little taste searched for a sense of themselves. The two lovers were here for the music. They were here to discover each other. They were alone in this dismal place with nothing but a sense of the past to guide them. When jazz is in the air the possibilities are endless, magic, lightning may strike at any moment.

There are certain truths that stand the test of time. To refer to these truths as cliché is dismissive. The best laid plans of mice and men are always to be disrupted in due time; Murphy's law always holds true. The evening of the second date between Matthias and his lovely young lady had been no different. The original plan was for a double date to the jazz show down in gas-town. Unforeseen circumstances, beneficial to all parties involved in the end, had arisen and the night was set on it's head. A foursome had become a twosome, Matthias prepared himself for the inevitable cancellation of the evening and sent his date a text message detailing the events. His heart clenched for the duration of the lingering moments between texts. There is a moment of anticipation just before the incoming message is read that plays havoc with the mind. A racing of thoughts that deny and confirm the worst of our nightmares. *She's not coming now. She's going to cancel on me. What do I do now? How should I handle this?* Matthias's mind raced through the endless possibilities of negative outcomes to this scenario only to find that upon reading the response to his message that everything was still on for the evening and the cancellation of his two friends had not swayed the young beauty from attending the evening concert with him. There was still a chance that the romantic endeavour would blossom their budding friendship into so much more as he had hoped. So many late nights lying awake dreaming of the words to speak, to write, to unleash the passion that he had seen within her beautiful brown eyes. *Am I just imagining that I saw that look in her eyes the other night? I don't think so. Is she just a friend? Does she love me? Is she thinking the same thing right now, at this very moment?* Questions beget questions, and the mind of a confused lover becomes muddier.

The evening began with a walk from the train station through the empty streets of Gas-town. The two, just a little nervous, still feeling each other out set forth toward the venue for the evening. Along the way it was mere coincidence that they discovered a quaint little French restaurant where the atmosphere for the night would take a beneficial turn. They talked over glasses of red wine and a blended brie and edam cheese fondue with a hint of white wine. The conversation, much as on the first date, was beyond natural. The two were so in sync with each other that it was obvious to everyone in the room that they were a couple even before they knew they were.

When the concert ended Matthias flagged down a cab for them having noticed that she was beginning to shiver at the cold night breeze that was stirring up. They hopped into the taxi and began to drive along when fate stepped in. Noticing that his lady was still cold Matthias decided to finally make a bold move, the first of many, and pulled her body to his cradling her for warmth. She did not resist. She placed a cold hand on the inside of his upper arm for his body heat to warm her. Her head nestled gently toward his chest as his arm pulled her in tight to him. There was a moment of quiet comfort. For the first time on either of their encounters the conversation had finally come to a halt and they were comfortable together in silence.

As Matthias walked home along the shore of the beach his resolve began to grow with the events of the evening unfolding before his eyes. This was real. The first night together had been amazing with neither wanting to go home until the inevitable had to happen and they parted rather awkwardly with a cab taking her off into the night. Tonight was different. Everything had magically fallen in place and they were closer than ever to becoming that something special that he felt in his heart. Love had grown between them on this night. Matthias smiled brightly for the first time in a long time and knew deep down in his heart that second chances were indeed possible. Her song was filling him with every step. Her smile forever etched into his eyes, into his mind, into the music of his heart.

Volume 3

VOLUME 3 CONTENTS

AN INTRODUCTION
TO VOLUME 3

It is a very rare thing in this life that we are given second chances. I am a very lucky man. To have been given this opportunity, to have fallen in love with my beautiful S____, it is truly something from a dream. She is my everything. The sun shines because of her. She lights up my eyes every time I see her, every time I hear her voice, and every time I smell her perfume. This collection of poems and stories is dedicated to the growing love that we have shared to this point in our budding relationship and to the glorious future that awaits us.

April 4th

On this of all mornings, it is fitting that the sun
Has never shone so brightly, that the birds
Have not whistled so sweet a tune as that which
Now tickles my senses,
My eyes wide open to the gifts of this magnificent day,
For today I am alive with the beat of love in my heart,
A spring in my step at the sound of your voice,
And I am one with the world around me.

On this of all mornings, it is of little surprise that
There is a smile on my face, that my stylus quivers
Between my thumb and forefinger,
Itching to pen my inspired thoughts and amorous feelings,
To make record of the glorious nature of this magnificent
day,
As if it were meant to be, like the night that
The stars fell in line for you and I,
It is of no great wonder that the sun would shine so
brightly for us today.

WHEN I HOLD YOU
IN MY ARMS

My scattered thoughts run rampant through my head,
This early morning has not been kind to the weary,
Those in need of rest, I lay me down upon my pillow
In search of quiet slumber and find my eyes wide open,
My ears pricked up scanning the silence for a trace of your
sound,
My fingers grasping at the air before them while the last
remnant
Of your sweet perfume still sees fit to tickle my nose,
Every sense in tune, seeking that which is missing,
Which should be here with me, that which completes me,
In order to make me go to sleep and dream my dreams of
possible futures,
With a smile on my face, my love by my side always and
forever,
Surrounded by your grace at every turn,
But today I shall sleep alone, a restless disjointed affair,
Tossing and turning away the hours of the day,
Counting the minutes until I can see you again,
Basking in your warm glow, breathing in your sweet
perfume,
Your hand clasped tightly in mine, sharing a laugh,
Pillow talk moments of silly splendour as we always do,
And I feel at home again, for I love you and all of your
charms,
And I will never be able to sleep the same when I am
alone,
Not the same as when I hold you in my arms.

Through My Eyes

I take this moment, these precious few minutes,
With pen and paper in hand, thoughts plucked from my
mind,
To attempt to explain a picture, a portrait of my love,
Of my sweet S_____, my sleeping angel,
So may my words be swift, and the sentiment be swaying,
May they clearly illustrate that which I feel in my heart,
That which pounds through me with every single beat,
Which flows through my veins,
fills my lungs, feeds my artistic mind,
And satisfies my romantic soul,
So let me scribe the story of my sleeping beauty,
Her soft skin, her sultry lips,
Her eyes shut tight from the glow of the moonlight
Reflecting off of the majestic mountain lake outside of our
window,
My arms wrapped around her waist, across her breast,
My lips gently kissing her neck, her ear lobe,
Whispering wanting words and secret whims,
Daring to dream of a future where we can lay together
Without worry of outside worlds,
Garrulous gaggles of silly strangers that flock like geese,
Clicking their sharp little tongues so flippantly,
Attempting to cut the strings connecting our hearts
With their destructive dialogue,
Dreaming of days in the sun walking hand in hand on
white sand beaches,

The soapy waves washing over our feet,
Where every step into the future is ours and ours alone,
The summer breeze blowing the perfumed blossoms
Of our delicious thoughts back to us for the next moment
to arise,
Of nights where we dine under a soft glowing moon,
The seamless sky above, scattered stars laid out before us,
Like a mystical map of treasures unknown,
Waiting for two lovers to reach up and grasp at them,
Take hold of their celestial secrets and create a
Bold and brighter tomorrow for those that they love,
And so . . . In that moment,
with my words whispering whims
Across your sweet soft neck, my arms grasping hold of
you,
Never wanting to let go, I made a choice,
A decision to share the moment with you from where I
stood,
To allow you this opportunity to see the future that I see
Every time I see your smile, every time you say my name,
Every time your beautiful brown eyes look upon me,
To show you that, in this moment, I am floating on a
cloud of your love,
Caught in a peaceful slumber, a wonderful waking dream,
One in which I wish to remain forever,
For the rest of my life, with you by my side,
And so . . . My beautiful angel,

I released my arms from around your form,
Kissed your brow and ran my fingers through your hair,
Slid myself slowly from your side and took this picture for
you,
This glimpse of my every hope and dream,
This portrait of the most amazing woman that I have ever
known,
As an attempt to show you the love that I feel for you
Every moment of every day, a chance to see through my
eyes,
To see how lovely you really are,
How peaceful, how beautiful my dreams can be,
And to allow you the opportunity to see
Just how much I love you.

SYMPHONY

I see you everywhere,
I feel you under my skin,
Rain or shine, my girl,
You are always on my mind,

Your smile lights up my sky,
Your eyes like magic,
Guiding me through the darkest night,
Into the bright future,

Every morning when I wake,
Your voice dances through my head,
Always in my heart,
Your laughter, a sweet song of love,

And I know, for all time,
With every ounce of blood
That flows through my veins,
From head to toe,

You are the one for me,
And I, so madly in love with you,
Will always hear this song
This symphony of love,

For I see you everywhere,
I feel you under my skin,
Rain or shine, my girl,
You are always on my mind.

THANKFUL

With each new day, the rising sun,
The morning breeze, the sweet harmonious song
Cascading from the trees all around us,
We've so much to be thankful for,
So many wonders to fill our hearts,
And engage our minds,
A bounty of treasures to remain with us
And all the time in the world to enjoy them
If we take but a moment to rest our bodies,
And quiet our thoughts,
Slow down the day and get caught up
In the magic that surrounds us,
For we should be so lucky,
To live but a moment,
In this wonderful world of ours.

TOMORROW

The raindrops roll down my cheek
From cold and dampened hair,
The light drizzle of this early evening
Has accumulated into a drenching dreamscape
In which I gaze across the horizon,
Pondering my private hopes of the future,
A picture perfect painting of watercolour wishes,
Lingering on the lips of a man in love,
Standing alone tonight,
On the edge of the evening,
With my girl on my mind,
The world, wet at my fingertips
As the sun slowly sinks from the sky,
And the moon begins to smile from behind a cloud,
A new day lingers around the corner,
With a new sun, where second chances are born,
And true love will always live on the lips
Of those with passion in their hearts,
And in their kiss.

ON THIS DAY

May it be, that on this day,
I have witnessed a change in the air,
The bitter cold has withdrawn,
The sunshine bright and bold has burst
Through the clouds and the birds are singing,
Once more, a familiar tune,
A song of spring that jumps into your heart,
Grabs hold of your spirit and dances until the moon
begins to rise.

Yes, may it be, that on this day,
I have risen from my sleeping pose and embraced,
With arms spread wide, the morning sun shining
Spectacularly through my window,
Placing a spring in my step,
Coupled with a song in my heart
Provided solely by the lips of an angel
And the raw emotions that only her smile can stir within me.

So, may it be said, that on this day,
I have taken a vow based on the ever present love
That grows daily within my heart,
To spend each and every moment of my precious future,
Making my girl happy, my one and only,
My true love,
For on this day I have witnessed the majesty of the mountains,
The breathtaking beauty of the ocean,
And the awe inspiring spring blossoms in the trees,
And none of these amazing things
Will ever pull at my heart strings the way that she does.

AS YOU LAY SLEEPING

My dearest love, I write to you now,
As you lay sleeping, your beautiful body next to mine,
The warmth of your skin, your soft slender form
Pressed tightly to me, and I am enamoured,
Restless tonight to tell you all of the
Hopes and dreams within my heart,
To express the endless joy that envelops me
At the very mention of your name,
How it rolls so sweetly from my tongue,
I am alive, living every moment you are near me
To the absolute fullest,
My lips still burning from your kiss,
My eyes taking in your every move, always remembering,
The sensation of your touch forever on my mind,
And I take this moment to write these words
As you lay sleeping right here beside me,
My dearest love, to attempt to tell you in my clumsy way,
That I am the luckiest man alive,
Because I am here with you, together tonight,
With the future before us, as we,
One kiss at a time, continue to fall,
Even deeper in love.

The Promise

Last night, at long last, or so it seems,
After several days of separation,
We shared our souls once more,
Our secrets spoken in soft whispers,
Safe within our strong embrace,
Your heart beating in tune with mine,
Pressed together in this pose,
This perfect moment in which I promised,
My precious angel, that I will always be here for you,
All that I am, every little piece of me is
Forever dedicated to your happiness,
To the preservation of your smile,
To always ease your mind from worry,
To comfort you, to hold you close to me,
To protect you at all times,
To always entreat you to the tale of how you
First came to steal my heart,
Of how my every breath, since our first embrace,
Is dedicated to you my lovely lady,
Your caring heart fills me every second of every day,
So many thoughts of you, my every dream,
One by one, as if by magic,
Slowly coming true, my life so full of joy,
Of wonder, the promise that the sun will shine tomorrow,
That all of my desires, my passions, my prose,
Will not linger long within limbo, that they too
Shall be loosed upon this world to be savoured,
Just as I savour each moment I am with you,
And I promise, with all sincerity and the utmost certainty,

That our story, the tale of two lovers from different
worlds,
Will continue to write itself as it has so far,
The pitfalls, the perils, the laughter, the love,
Twisting and turning,
Weaving a spell that we have both fallen under,
Happily ever after.

THIS WAKING DREAM

You have saved me, your comforting,
Soothing sound has brought me back home,
Your voice like a guiding star has stolen me from
This waking dream, from the savage anguish
That I felt deep down in the pit of my stomach,
The bottomless, ever dropping, sadistic sensation,
From this horrid dream, this nightmarish reality,
This harrowing harbinger in which I, helpless,
Lay powerless, stretching my hands outward,
Reaching to you, so far away,
Unable to grasp you and pull you to me,
Unable to assuage the pain that you were feeling,
Unable to ease your suffering,
A torturous torment created deep within my brain,
A warning that I must heed, whatever does it mean,
My love, in order to free myself of this falling feeling,
I must decipher this waking dream and
Stop this foreboding dread.

You have saved me, for mere minutes ago,
Trapped within a hellish sleep I lay restless,
Tossing and turning to the tempest of
A collective hopeless hurricane within my mind,
A foreboding feeling that I will not be
Able to reach to you in a moment of need,
That the distance between us in the physical world,
The unwanted spaces, on this night that we're apart,
Are too much for me to bridge with mere words,
That I will not be able to soothe your troubled thoughts,
That my hands will not be able to stroke your hair,

That my arms will not be able to wrap themselves
Around you and hold you tightly to my breast,
Safe and secure, warm within this embrace,
Wearing my love for you like a blanket,
But then you saved me from this waking dream,
Your voice piercing the darkness like a beacon of light,
For it was I this time that needed to hear your words,
And feel your love, because it eases my mind,
And rests my troubled thoughts,
On this lonely night without you,
And now I am safe.

Secret Thoughts

I don't know what to say, what it was that brought me this
way,
The soft breeze blowing through my window,
The slow setting sun, the time away from my love,
Her face forever before my eyes,
Her warm embrace always on my mind,
I have wandered my way here,
A wayward pace to this moment in time,
My feet set firmly in the sand,
The gentle waves rushing onto the beach in minute swells,
Glistening in their stillness,
I can see my hopes and dreams of the past rising once
more,
Light hearted childish fare from days gone by,
Peaceful and serene, a quiet reminder,
A footprint in the sand telling me
That I am once again upon the path that I was meant to
tread,
No-longer a lonely traveler,
My guide, a set of beautiful brown eyes,
A smile that swells my heart and sets my soul on fire,
And I am certain that this time,
With every breath, you are in my blood,
The future, once so daunting,
now a tamed and timid tiger whose stripes,
Once a mystery, are now so easily read,
Like my once secret thoughts, kept only for me,
Now laid softly upon your sweet, soft, neck
Each and every night that we are together,
Building a life for us, one thought,

One kiss, one night, one day at a time,
So that we may look back at moments like these,
Sitting on a log on the beach,
Watching the sunset,
And remember the sights and the sounds,
The smells and the touches,
The tastes of a life built step by step,
Brick by brick,
With the magic of our love.

THE WHY OF IT

I wait for you, out here amongst the concrete and steel,
The towering atrocities blocking the landscape,
The roaring thunder of urban Thursday nights,
So cold and callous, the day to day grind,
The burrowing banality that leans forth with
Lecherous fingers of friendship,
Bating and prodding, rubbing elbows and patting backs,
Determined to ensnare me, setting traps,
Attempting to tickle my senses,
But I stay true to my course, un-deterred,
Unafraid, my focus always on my girl,
And so I sit here tonight, on this street-side perch,
Amongst the neon nightlife, flashing past,
Always in a hurry to catch the next willing victim,
I sit here and wait for you, for a moment to hold you,
For a kinetic kiss, where our lips lock for a lifetime
Within a few seconds flushing our cheeks and
Quickening the beat of our hearts, setting the night on
fire,
Waiting here to look into your eyes and feel the
Warmth of your caring ways,
To tell you how much I love you, just one more time
today,
Simply because I need to, no rhyme or reason,
Nothing more than a feeling that runs through my veins
Every moment of every day,
And that is the why of it,
That is my heart, and it beats for you alone.

WHEN TOMORROW COMES

On this restless evening, I lay in waiting,
Scanning my surroundings, surveying,
Seeing that which has been a part of my life,
A part of my past, still present around me,
That which has been, has it served its purpose?,
Is the time at hand to lay these memories to rest?,
Once and for all time?, need I ask this question?,
As I scan this room my eyes don't know these things,
They don't feel like they belong, or better yet,
I don't feel like I belong here amongst them,
This truth is known deep within my heart,
My real happiness, my real home,
Is with my S____, she is the source of my greatest joy,
My comfort, and the true feeling of home,
And yet this place is bereft of this feeling,
There is but a small place for you here,
That which I have recently created,
And this is the reminder, here on this restless evening,
When my arms are so empty, I sit and I stare at these
walls,
Without recognition, this place, my home,
Is no-longer my home,
It is nothing more than an archive of the past,
A distant memory that I wish to remove from my daily
life,
And so I look toward the future,
Forward into dreams of a new home,
A place where we can be safe together,
Where the joy that your smile brings to me
Is apparent in everything around me,

Where I can feel you when you aren't with me,
And I know that I am safe,
But for now I am saddened that this reality
Is not yet within my grasp,
And tonight with empty arms, and restless thoughts,
I long for your touch, for you to be here with me,
To walk with me on my way,
But when tomorrow comes I will step confidently
Into my new life, toward the future,
With my dreams to be built around us,
One step at a time, for you deserve this and more from me
my love,
And so do I.

WHEN WE ARE TOGETHER

The possibilities of the future, so vast,
So expansive, so hard to grasp,
The intangible dream, so far away,
And yet at times so near
that my fingertips itch at the sensation,
If I could just stretch my hand that much further,
Reach beyond my arms length,
And capture that which eludes me,
That which is only so much closer to me
When we are together,
My resolve much stronger,
My mind and body as one,
Focused on tomorrow,
And I can see that which I could only see
In my dreams, in days gone by,
When I hold you in my arms I am alive,
And I can accomplish anything.

My Lovely Lady

Soft and sweet, your savoury skin,
Like silk, so sumptuous,
I slide my fingers along your spine,
A scholar in the science of love,
Studying the scripture of your
Supine form splayed out before me,
A sensuous song slipping from your
Lips as you say "Baby . . . I love you".

I stay my touch for a single moment,
Searching your seductive eyes,
Succumbing to the splendour of your
Sagacious words, your subtle,
Spontaneous kisses of salivary delight,
Sweeping you into my arms,
Submersing myself on this celebratory sojourn,
And I am satisfied, sleeping soundly
In the sanctuary of your arms.

A New Sunrise

My daring didactic diatribe,
Now double timed,
Skipping, twirling, tongue tied
Rhymes that lead and linger,
Falter and mingle with the sadness
That rests in my soul,
Capturing my mind, stealing away
With a teasing abhorred show,
Leading me away from tomorrow.

I dance and I sing my sarcastic song
Sadly through the night
But by the dawn,
With all curtains drawn
I find a startling sight,
A harmony that breaks my hatred down
And beckons me to follow
Into the bright and satisfying
Light of this new day sun.

Our Pleasurable Paradise

Let us play, taunt one-another with our
Seductive words and longing stares,
Pillow talking, pillow biting, verbs and feathers
In flight, a virtual playground
Of the delights of our bodies and minds
Together as one as we slowly fall into
The satin sheets of our pleasurable paradise,
On this magical evening under the stars,
Where the moon may be plucked from the sky
At any moment so that I may place it within
Your palm with a promise for the future,
Where you and I wander in wistful steps
Along sandy beaches, and your lips are kissing mine
Every night as we lay sleeping
Heart to heart, forever in love.

<u>Near Or Far</u>
<u>(Always With You)</u>

Do I dare to dream about you?,
To whisper words into the air,
With hopes that they may seem
To fly up through my window,
Rustle a few leaves in a nearby tree,
Dance with the moon in the starlight,
And free the celestial bodies of their nightly slumber,
Waken the world with the love that
Burns so brightly between us,
An endless flame that engulfs our bodies,
Making us one, so that night and day,
Whether you are near, or far away,
My touch will always be upon you,
My words within your thoughts,
And my kiss, floating softly on the breeze
Tonight, shall always find your cheek,
And so . . . I ask once more,
Do I dare to dream about you?,
To whisper my words on this night,
Alone and thinking of you,
Of course I do, because
You are always on my mind,
The beating in my heart,
And the air that fills my lungs,
But mostly because I love you S___,
And I don't like being without you.

I Dare Not Wake

Am I dreaming?, is this real,
These feelings that I feel?,
I dare not pinch myself for fear
That I may wake,
That my heart may be stolen
From this state of love and trust
That we have built between us,
That the smile that lights up my life
May disappear from before my eyes,
That my arms that hold you tightly
Throughout the night may suddenly
Be empty of your beautiful form.

Am I dreaming?, I know that this is real,
That for the past few months
I have become a better man,
More determined and full of fire,
Bursting forth, my passion and desire,
My creative mind unleashed once more,
To be with you,
To make a world where I may hold
You everyday, where love is less a secret
And more a bedtime tale told to children,
Blankets pulled tightly up to their necks
In cozy comfort, ready to dream
Of a love much like ours.

I know that I am not dreaming,
The love that I feel for you is real,
And I am certain,
Beyond a shadow of a doubt,
That when I kiss you,
The flutter in my heart,
The tingle down my spine will always
Be there each and every time
That we lock our lips together,
And far off down the road,
In another time,
We will look back at our beautiful beginnings,
Though we had times of struggle,
And our hearts will warm with the memory,
While I hold you in my arms,
And we'll both know that this is real.

WHEN LOVE DOESN'T
SEEM LIKE ENOUGH

Life is what we make of it,
Sometimes it's hard to see the end result
Of any given situation,
The strands of too many unfinished labours
Dangling before your eyes,
Knotted up into a large ball within your brain,
Forever weighing upon your mind,
Your heart,
Impacting the simple decisions from day to day,
Causing an unrest in your soul,
That threatens to steal your sanity.

I know all of this,
I have been here before,
Stuck somewhere between dreams and reality,
Where every desire in your heart
Seems so far away,
Just barely out of reach only a moment before,
The pressures of your daily life
Always upon your shoulders,
Ever present, without surcease,
To the point where you need to break away.

I know all of this and more,
For so many years I have lived within these walls,
Searching for the exit,
The doorway to my dreams,
And then I found you,

And although the strands of the unfinished
Still remain before me,
Their burden has become less stifling
When you are with me,
And I know that I'm just a penniless poet,
That my words are not what you're looking for,
That sometimes you feel like love just isn't enough,
Like you need protection from the harsh reality
Of an unknown tomorrow,
But my love, the sky will not fall.

I know all of these things,
And I know what's in your heart,
And as much as it pains me to do so,
To see you suffer like this,
With all of my love for you,
I am powerless to save you from this torment,
I must stand back,
Support you from afar
While you work things out for yourself,
But know this one thing
My dear and precious S____,
You are not alone in this,
not alone in anything you do,
For I will never leave you,
And though you think that
Love is not enough,

I will show you just how much
Real love can be worth,
That is why I am here,
The Huma bird has flown,
The tide is slowly turning in your favour,
Hold on just a little bit longer my love,
Trust me, it will be worth it.